On the Quiver of Mystery

Pastoral Poems
in Four Quarter Time

Robert VerEecke S.J.

© Copyright 2021 by Robert F. VerEecke S.J.

ISBN 978-0-578-85577-6

On the Quiver of Mystery:
Pastoral Poems in Four Quarter Time

ALL RIGHTS RESERVED

Cover Photo by Robert VerEecke
Day's Dawning over Brace Rock
Eastern Point Retreat House

Additional Photos can be seen at:
robertvereecke.org

Designed and Printed by Paraclete Multimedia

CONTENTS

INTRODUCTION   5

All A Quiver FOR GERARD MANLEY HOPKINS   9

Quiver 1
AUTUMN/ ORDINARY TIME

Going Poem Picking	13
Over the Moon	14
Seas the Day! Three Day Nor'Easter	16
PSS (Post Storm Script)	19
Gully Gee	20
Tea for Two	22
Luke and See	24
The Prayer- We Breathe	27
Cache or Credit?	28
Autumn Weaves	29
Autumn Belief	30
Aye, Aye!	31
Autumn's End	32
More Prose than Cons	34
Zach's Zounds	35
First Frost	36
Worth the Wave?	38
INRI	39

Quiver 2
WINTER/ ADVENT

On "That" Day	45
On "This" Day	46
The Baptist's Breach	47
Gobsmacked	48
Mary's Mind	50
Announcements	52
Mind Meld	54
Ask Me? Ask You?	56
What a Whirl!	58
Quite a Day!	60
Rendez-Vue	63
Sea Here	64
Cristal-Eyes	65

Quiver 3
SPRING/ LENT/EASTER

What a Whorl! ASH WEDNESDAY	70
Squirrel Scramble	72
The Band Played On	74
Wicked Good!	75
A Deer's Cry-In Hindsight	76
Stag Leap RAISING OF LAZARUS	78
Free for All PALM SUNDAY	79
God's Free Day GOOD FRIDAY	80
DNA EASTER SUNDAY	82
Twinning	83
Had	86
Come Back	88
Cobble's Tones PENTECOST	91
An Earful	93

Quiver 4
SUMMER/ ORDINARY TIME 2

Soul-Stice	97
A Paean for Peonies TRINITY SUNDAY	98
Clean Slate	99
Full Grown	101
A New Brew	102
Undertow	104
Day's Daze	107
Be Still!	109
Duple Time	110
All's Fare	111
Levi-Tation	114
To Know a Veil	116
What's Now	117
Enthralled	118
And How!	120

INTRODUCTION

Gonzaga Retreat House in Gloucester, Massachusetts, is situated on a promontory called Eastern Point. For more than 60 years, it has welcomed thousands of retreatants seeking silence and solace. For all who have come, this is "Holy Ground," and each person's soul is "set aquiver," encountering the mystery of God. Whether it be the sometimes turbulent, sometimes serene Atlantic Ocean; the majestic Brace Rock, a symbol of God's steadfastness; the waves that crash and break over the rock formations; the stunning sunrises over the Atlantic or sunsets over Niles Pond; the songs of birds and the caws of gulls, it does not take long for one to feel "all aquiver." And as one enters into the silence and surrounding sounds of creation and hears the voice of God in the scriptures and in prayer, the soul is set aquiver. "Sometimes it causes you to tremble, tremble, tremble…"

My own soul has been set aquiver countless times as a retreatant at Gonzaga Retreat House over the past 40 years. Now I am fortunate to live on this Holy Ground and direct retreats for those who are setting aside time in their busy lives for silence, prayer and conversation with God. In addition to my work as a retreat director and a blogger on the daily scriptures, I have been writing poems inspired by the seascape, the scriptures and the seasons. When I began writing poems in the autumn, I could never have imagined that winter, spring and summer would be marked with the suffering of a pandemic of epic proportions. We have been living "on the quiver of mystery" through most of this year 2020. And yet, as we tremble with our fear of the unknown, we are still called to enter into the Paschal Mystery, that profound promise of hope, redemption and God's eternal faithfulness.

Although my ordained ministry has brought me to serve in parishes and on a college campus, I have also been able to share my artistic gifts as a choreographer and teacher of dance. During my time as Jesuit Artist-in-Residence at Boston College I had the opportunity to work not only with students and alumni but also with professional dancers in the Boston and New York area. Every year for the past forty, I presented *A Dancer's Christmas*, heralded by the Boston Globe as "a religious alternative to the Nutcracker."

I believe that it is my expertise as a choreographer that has helped me to find my poetic voice. Readers will notice in the poems the sometimes smooth and sometimes jagged lines that capture the flow as well as angularity of movement expression. "Fall and recovery" being a primary technique of modern dance, I try to create rhythms that imitate this rising and falling. As a choreographer who loves the way one movement flows into another, I want my lines to do the same. Moreover, since movement often has a staccato feel to it, I look for unexpected stresses that serve as notational emphases in my poems. Since dance is a visual art form that also uses music and sound, I play with words that sound the same but have different meanings. That's why the poems need to be seen as well as heard! Although the poetic lines do not *follow a structured meter,* the "feet" are always at work in this choreographer's poetry.

As a Jesuit priest, I have been most influenced by the poetry of Gerard Manley Hopkins. The wordplay in his poems, their 'instress' and sprung rhythm, his finding God in all things and Christ as all in all, have captivated me from the first time I heard "Pied Beauty" as a high-school student. As a choreographer of dance, I often feel Hopkin's words dancing. Sometimes it's a slow pavane, but more often a galliard or gallop. Often when I write, I feel that he's looking over my shoulder and delighting with me as together we find the wonder of words. The first poem in this collection is my humble attempt to thank him for his ongoing inspiration.

The poet Mary Oliver has been another source of inspiration for me. The way she invites the reader to see creation with "crystal eyes," and describes it with her economy of words, inspires me not to be an "on-looker" but an "in-looker." "Going Poem Picking" was my first foray into writing, and I hope she would be delighted with its words and images if she were to read it.

I owe the title "On the Quiver of Mystery" to Paul Mariani and his book, *The Mystery of it All. The Vocation of Poetry in the Twilight of Modernity.* (Paraclete Press 2019). Mariani, a noted Hopkins scholar and poet himself, has remarkable insight not only into Hopkins's poetry but into the poet as well. The first section of his book, entitled "On the Quiver of Mystery," weaves an analysis of the beauty and depth of Hopkins's poetry with the mystery of one who calls himself "This Jack, joke, poor potsherd, patch, matchwood, immortal diamond." (*That Nature is a Heraclitean Fire and of the comfort of the Resurrection*).

On the Quiver of Mystery: Pastoral Poems in Four Quarter Time follows both the rhythm of the four seasons as well as the liturgical year. The poems are meant to be "pastoral": to open your mind and heart to the presence and action of God in your life. Almost all of them weave the scripture of the day and/or the liturgical feast with themes of creation, incarnation, human and divine suffering, and the paschal mystery. Those written during the pandemic of 2020 reference not only human suffering but also the question of God's providence in all that the world has experienced. "Four Quarter" refers not only to the four seasons but also the music and dance rhythms that I use. You may find a 2/4, 3/4, 4/4 rhythm that will make you want to dance! "What a Whirl," which was inspired by the passage of David dancing before the Ark, is a good example of how I use dance rhythms in many of the poems.

My hope is that the readers of these poems will be "all aquiver" as they delight with me in God's love for the world and the Word made flesh.

Robert F. VerEecke S.J.

All A Quiver
for GMH
Mark 9:14-29

Was it the bird songs
heard this Hopkins morning
that set my ears aquiver,
their quavering voices
lasting longer than a
quaver and me all aquiver?

Or was it the deciduous trees
seen this Hopkins morning
that set my mind's eye aquiver,
their branches bare,
baring themselves,
half-naked now
stripped of spring and summer
revealing patches of blue
with arms outstretched?

Or was it the sheep, the Scottish cow,
or the miniature mules
felt this Hopkins morning
that set my hands aquiver,
wanting to touch and feel their coats,
coarse and wooly, of course?
Were these creatures of our
God and King, key to my quivering?

Or was it the balsam wreaths,
with their Christmas scent
on this Hopkins morning
that set my soul aquiver?
The nose knows.
Noel swells anew
and I am all aquiver.

Or was it the Gospel
heard this Hopkins morning
that set my heart aquiver?
He draws from his quiver of stories,
not missing the mark
No *harmatia* here except
the sin of unbelief.

But who could blame a father,
seeing his son quivering and quaking?
But Jesus calms the storm
within and without, instressed
and outstretched, his heart
and the father's all aquiver.

Could it be that the Divine Marksman
was drawing from the quiver of creation,
shooting arrows of awe
as Hopkins himself heard and felt and saw?
A poet's Eros and A-gape?
And all is on the quiver of mystery!

AUTUMN 2019
Quiver 1

Going Poem Picking

for FRANCIS AND MARY
(Francis of Assisi and Mary Oliver)

I wish I could pick poems from bushes and brambles
Like berries in summer
Poems plump with pulpy words and juicy images
Bursting blues and blacks, rasping reds
Sweet and sour, these poems plucked.
An elder, berry wise would risk rambling in the brambles
Not whining about prickling thorns
But picking and plucking to her heart's content.

I wish I could pick poems from trees
Like apples in autumn
Poems ripe with delicious words and jazzy images
Polished pink and ruby red
Honey sweet vowels with crisp consonants.
A gala of golden poems
Falling, cascading like cataracts.
Better wear a Macintosh!

Over the Moon
for FRANCIS AND MARY

I can almost pinpoint brother Sun's rising on the horizon.
Surprising in colors and hues, yes, but guess the point?
No, I know where to look.
And brother Sun rarely disappoints
Even on cloudy, rainy days when sun is unseen
I know where to point.
That's the point isn't it?
Brother Sun is so, so, so consistent!
When it comes to brother Sun, I always know where to look
Living on the edge, as I do. The ocean's edge, that is.
O Sole Mio!

When it comes to sister Moon, it's another story.
She is always playing hide and seek!
I can never pin sister Moon's rising point.
It's pointless for me to even try.
She's always teasing me with her whereabouts.
Last night I went lunar looking and sky scanning
She was nowhere to be found until I heard her whisper
"Over here! You're searching for me in the wrong place!"
Sister Moon is so, so, so elusive!
With her waxing and waning, always going through phases, moth-like.
O Sola Luna!

Increase our faith, the apostles say!
Have they never seen the moon with her waxing and waning?
Don't they know that faith is no-thing, nothing quantifiable?
It's always waxing and waning, going through phases
"I believe, help my unbelief" "I believe, help my unbelief"
Faith's hiding, lunar like in the dark, no where-abouts to be seen, then
Making an appearance in an unexpected place.
It's a must see, the moon in all her fullness
If you have faith the size of mustard seed is a must see.
Does your God search need a good search of another Trinity?
The sun, the moon and
Oh! The stars!

Seas, the day!
(November Nor'easter)

Day 1
Malachi 3

Howling, harrowing, hammering,
Havoc wreaking wind!
Wailing, whistling, whining,
Whorl- whirling wind!
Blustering, blistering, blasting,
Blowing bellows-like wind!
Malachi-like, your voice
Shatters the silence.
Malachi-like your power
Churns, turns
Serene seas to stormy.
Seizing the seas
Seizing the day!
For lo! the day is coming,
Wailing like a whale
When all the proud and all the pompous
Will be rubble,
Leaving them neither driftwood,
(Handel-bars for riding the waves)
Nor buoys to hold on to.
Like sunken ships buried below,
While wind bellows above.
But for you who are in awe of God's creation,
Seas, the Day!

Day 2
Joel 1-2

Howling, harrowing, hammering.
Havoc wreaking wind!
Wailing, whistling, whining,
Whorl- whirling wind!
Blustering, blistering, blasting,
Blowing bellows-like wind!
Joel-like, your voice
Shatters the silence.
Joel-like your power
Churns, turns
Serene seas to stormy.
Seizing the seas
Seizing the day!
Gird yourselves and grab your galoshes, O people!
Whale of a gale out there!
Yes, it is here, a day grey with white board skies
That God could write on with magic markers,
With waves spuming and fuming over the rocks,
Breaking hearts hoping to sea, sunlight sparkling serenely
But No, ah, a nor'easter fully formed frightening the faint of heart.
It's like has not been from the days of Noah
No, ah, it will come to an end somewhere…
"Over the Rainbow"

Day 3
2 Kings 5

Howling, harrowing, hammering,
Havoc wreaking wind!
Wailing, whistling, whining,
Whorl- whirling wind!
Blustering, blistering, blasting,
Blowing bellows-like wind!
Elisha-like, your voice
Whips through the silence.
Elisha-like your power
Churns, turns
Serene skies to stormy.
Seizing the seas
Sizing the skies, the limit-less
Expanse of white,
Chalky white, writing the skies with invisible ink
Righting the skies and the seas.
Can you see God's handwriting,
Skywriting with Magic markers?
No chalk on blackboard but
Rather white on white, invisible to the I.
Naaman can see in the sinking down, down into the water,
Rising up with flesh as white as the whiteboard sky
No man, nor woman can be cast out
Into the deep but out of the depths
And into the depths of God's (dare I say)
Leprous love,
Contagious love whose wingspan,
Wind span is as limitless as
White skies, right skies, sky-writing
As far as I can see,
Seas, the day.
Skies, the limit.
But when, o when, o when,
I whine,
Will this storm be over?

Day 4
Luke 17: 11-19

PSS (Post Storm Script)

I wake to wonder
Where did it go?
That storm with its wailing winds,
With its tumult and turbulence
Whipping seas to creamy crests,
Crescendos of sound
Lashing out, unleashing nature's fury.

In the storm's wake
Whispering winds,
Caressing limbs and branches
Broken and twisted in the storm.
Diminuendos of sound
Soft, muted, pianissimo
One has to strain to hear.

I wake to see
Surfers skimming the surface of the lawn
With boards under their arms,
Racing to reach the sea, to catch the
   waning waves.
The white board sky is now
Blue on blue with streaks of yellow/red/orange
Pre-script for sunrise, post-script for
   grey skies.

I wake to wonder
Where did it go?
My storm with its woes and worries,
With its tempests and terrors,
Whipping me with its lashes
Crescendos of sound,
"Unclean!, Unclean!"
Keep your distance and disdain!

In the storm's wake,
Now only the voice of Jesus
Whispering words,
Caressing limbs
Broken and twisted by life's leprosy.
"Go and show yourself!"
The show must go on!

In the storm's wake
All is calm, all is bright
No more whining,
Only bread and wining.
Eucharist
You carry us,
God of storm, sea and sky
Jesus, healing word and
Self-giving sacrament,
And we give thanks.

Gully Gee!

When will I tire of seeking sunrise?
Each morning I wonder,
"Will it be worth the wait?
Will I see painterly skies,
a palette of purple hues,
mauves and magentas.
lavenders and lilacs?
Or a palette of other hues
ruby, raspberry, rose reds,
burnt orange or burnished yellow?"

On the Vereeckter scale, from 1 to 10
yesterday's sunrise scored 8.
High praise! High marks!
Glorious!
Golly Gee!
Good going God!

On the Vereeckter scale, from 1-10
today's sunrise scores 5.
So, so,
ho-hum,
hum-drum,
nothing worth waiting for.

And then, the "caw" of a gull calling!
Chastising me,
"Judge not, lest you be judged!"
The gall of the gull!
And I blushed with hues of sunrise
Purple, red and orange,
Because she was right!
Who am I to judge?
Who am I to be creation's critic?
Who am I anyway?
And then a whole colony of gulls, "cawing"
(or was it God in de skies?)
"Be grateful that you have eyes to see sea and sunrise!"
Gully Gee!

Tea for Two
Memorial of Teresa of Avila

Imagine a tea for two.
Two women,
Teresa and Mary,
Wit and wisdom.
Which one wit?
Which wisdom?
Both/and another thing….
Two women,
Living centuries apart, yet
Together, one mind, one spirit.
They speak with the gift of tongues
Each in her own language
Ambos se entienden,
Understand each other
Both/and another thing…
Teresa "avails" herself of prose,
She a mystic rose.
Mary, "a lover" of poetry
She a mystic muse.
Patience and Prayer
Mary patching a few words together,
Thatched prayer. God's roofing for us.
Teresa daring to dance while waiting patiently
Hatching prayer
La incubación de la oración
Nada te turbe
Let nothing disturb you

Two women
One mind, one spirit
Both/and another thing…
Creation and Compassion
Mary muses,
Seeing God in all
Embracing all in all
Poem of the One World
Teresa medita,
Mirando a Dios en todo
Abrazando todo en todo
Dios está en el camino con nosotros
Two women,
A weaving of wit and wisdom
A meeting of minds
Tea for Two?

Luke and See
Feast of St Luke

Can you see Luke
Putting pen to parchment,
Inscribing stories,
Telling tales to Theophilus,
Lover of God,
Tales told by women who witnessed wonders
Mother Mary, Martha, Magdalene ,
Those Christophilai
Lovers of Christ Jesus?
Luke and see!

Can you see Luke
Putting pen to parchment
Story telling?
Angel announcing,
Zachariah zapped,
A moot point!
Angel announcing,
Mary marveling,
A pregnant pause!
Angel announcing,
Elizabeth elated,
A jumping Jack!
Luke and see!

Can you see Luke
Putting pen to papyrus
Story telling?
Angels announcing,
Astonishing shepherds
Flocking with sleepy sheep
To look and see
A creche child, the Christ-child?
Luke and see!

Can you see Luke
Putting pen to parchment,
Penning parables
Prodigally?
"There was a man who had two sons…"
"There was a man going down from Jerusalem to Jericho…"
"There was a rich man, who was clothed in purple…"
Scribing stories,
Women-wise, women's ways
A woman anointing
A widow weeping
A woman sweeping
A widow persisting
Luke and see!

Can you see Luke
Penning the story,
Short-limbed Zaccheus,
Climbing a long limbed
Tree just to see Jesus
Going for a glimpse
And getting so much more
than a sycamore?
Luke and Laugh!

Can you see Luke
Putting pen to papyrus
Writing roadways?
The road to Jerusalem
The road to Calvary
The road to Emmaus
Two disciples
Bread Breaking
Hearts Burning
Eyes Opening
Luke and See!

The Prayer – We Breathe
Luke 18:1-8

Autumn Air
Brisk, bracing
Crisp, cooling
Fall feeling
Pleasing?
Breathe in
Spiro
Breathe out
Spero

Autumn Prayer
Brisk, bracing
Crisp, cooling
Feel falling
A widow's pleas?
A widow's might?
God's widowing,
Winnowing?
Who's to judge?
Pr-air in
Spiro
Pr-air out
Spero

Autumn Prayer
Air on a C string of colors
Russet, remembering
Amber, asking
Yellow, yearning
Purple, pleading
People pleasing
Leave it to Autumn!
Is prayer "pleas-ing?"
You be the judge!

Breath in
Spiro
Breath out
Spero

Dum Spiro, Spero
While I breathe, I hope.

Cache or Credit?
Luke. 12:13-21

Quite a cache!
    Where house my wares?
        Some safe place no one knows.
           A barn?
Barns burn, too many bales
    A building?
        Buildings buckle, too many stories
           A vault?
                Of course!
           Vaults hold hidden treasures
           No safer place than a vault
           No stealing from this steel
              Vault-less no longer!
        I take all the credit for my cache!

Foolish, frivolous,
    Feckless fellow!
        A vault for your vanity!
           Housing, hording, hiding
                Heaven's treasures,
                      God's gifts!
                            Better credit God, than cache.
              Here's the catch.
              With God,
            No need for a vault,
        There's the vault of the sky.
              With God,
        No need for a warehouse
    When a small wooden box holds
            the universe.

Autumn Weaves
St Anthony Claret
WEAVER

If I were a weaver
I'd be an eager one
An eager weaver
Busy at my loom
Criss crossing colors
Fiery reds
Burnt oranges
Glowing ambers
Beaver-like I'd weave
With yarns of yearning
Not sticks and branches
My warp and weft
But hopes and dreams
Fiery red
Burnt orange
Glowing amber
And not give a damn
About what looms ahead.

If I were a weaver
I'd be an eager one
An eager weaver
Like Jesus was
Criss-crossing
Cana and Capernaum
Judea and Jerusalem
Weaving words of God's reign
His warp and weft
Justice and compassion
Fiery words, ablaze and aglow.
He did not give a damn
About the Christ Cross that
loomed ahead.

If I were a weaver
I'd be a busy one.
A busy weaver
Like Paul was
Christ-crossing
Sin, slavery
Salvation, sanctification.
Weaving words in Christ
Death-defying
His warp and weft
Freedom and Forgiveness
Fierce and fiery words
A blaze of glory
No damming God's grace
In Jesus Christ.

If you wonder if God's a weaver
Just behold the autumn leaves:
Fiery red
Burnt orange
Glowing amber
Criss-crossing colors
Christ-crossing
At warp speed!

Autumn Belief

For the faithful departed

Ought I be leaving in Autumn?
Ought I take my leave,
fatefully departing,
leaving leaf-like,
no longer clinging
to bough and branch of life,
fading, falling earth-wise,
one among so many?
No more.

Ought leaves be leaving in Autumn?
They do not decide for themselves,
these deciduous leaves.
their time to depart is fated
soon to be faithful departed,
no longer clinging
to bough or branch.
They let go after a short-lived life.
Three seasons
No more?

Ought leaves be leaving in Autumn?
Their work is done,
once shades of green,
shading, sheltering,
now shades of red, yellow and orange
gracious and glorious
and then, fading, falling, earth wise.
No more.

Do trees bend and bow out of respect for
leaves loved,
lives lived?
Do branches and boughs break,
broken-hearted,
pining for leaves lost
lives lived?

Ought I be learning
from the leaves of Autumn
believing in,
every leaf, every life,
faithfully a part of the circle,
the cycle of living and dying?
No more!

Aye, Aye!
Romans 8:18-25

I eye the sea
Hi! sea, I say.
High seas, I see.
Storm churns,
Turns, topsy-turvy.
See for yourself, sea says.

I'm all eyes and ears, I say
Aye, Aye! sea says
High C's, I hear
Sea sings,
Scales, from sea to C
Hear for yourself, sea says.

Are you groaning? I ask.
Your high seas sound
Pain-filled like high C's
Off-key, more screech
than reached.
Labor pains, sea says
All creation contracting,
expanding, labor pangs.
Don't you see, sea says?
Your pain is mine
My pangs are yours.

Aye, Aye, I say,
Yes, sea, I see.
Not you or me but
We as one,
Reaching high, see?

Autumn's End
Romans 8:26-30

How ought I pray at autumn's end?
Is autumn's prayer seasoned differently?

Spirit sighs and says,
"Autumn's all about endings, isn't it?
Winter's waiting
Spring's awakening
Summer's ripening
Autumn leaves something to be desired.
What do you desire when all you see in autumn is endings?"

I sigh and say,
"Leaves falling, branches baring
Empty spaces in open air.
Where there was greening, grinning grass
Now browning, frowning,
No longer mown but moan
No longer grown but groan
My spirit is like the grass that fades,
The forgotten fruit that withers on the vine,
The falling leaves lying on beds of death and decay
My prayer futile, not fertile.
Is this how I ought to pray at autumn's end?"

Spirit sighs and says,
"Open your eyes!
Autumn is seasoned with hope.
Without the dying and decay
There would be no way
For winter's waiting,
For spring's awakening,
For summer's ripening.
How ought you pray at autumn's end?
Hopefully!"

More Prose than Cons
Romans 8:28

What if X had never happened?
    What would your life be like now?
X marks the spot when and where life changed.
    For better or for worse?
At first, for worse.
    The anguish and distress
The perilous sword of betrayal
    The famine of friends, forgetting
Your past, alone in the present,
    A futile future.
Wish X never was?

                X marks the spot
          When and where a chasm opened up
            Swallowing, separating you
              From past and future,
              Only pain present.
               Wish X never was?
            Wondering why X ever was?
              For better or for worse.
                Vows are made,
                Life's avowal, Yes
              But no, a consonant
          Sounding more prose than "con"
       "If God is for us, who can be against us?"

What if X had never been?	Christ,
What would your life be like now?	Bridging the chasm,
X marks the one	Christ,
Who changed the world to better!	Consonant
Cons to prose, Praise Him!	Christ,
X is key, X is chi	Love's avowal
Chi is Christ	Alpha and Omega,
Christ is key	All in all, more prose than cons
No longer "unknown"	"All things work for good for those who love God."

Zach's Zounds

Luke: 19:1-10

"Zounds!" says Zach,
"Rabbi's coming back.
Last time, missed him
Lost him in the crowd
This time, climb a tree
Get a glimpse now."

"Zounds!" says Zach,
"Not sure I have the knack
Those limbs may limp
Those boughs may break
My limbs too short
To climb a big mistake?

What the Gehenna!
Give it a try
Climb a sycamore
How and why?
Nothing more to lose
I've lost it already
Everyone despises me
'Cause I got plenty."

"Zounds!", says Zach
"He's turning around
This time sees me
Jeez, I've been found."
"Z'up?" Jeez says,
Sees me up in that tree.
"You're all wound up
You're wounded I see"
"Zounds!" says Zach,
"The way his voice sounds
You'd think he wanted
me hanging around."
"Yup," Jeez says,
"Do come down from that tree.
Dinner at your house,
Just you and me."

"What the Gehenna!"
Some gawkers say,
"He eats with sinners!
Jeez! Us — no way!
The law's the law
And it's very clear
Those people like shorty
You can't go near."

"Zounds!" says Zach,
standing his ground,
"Half my possessions
I'll spread them around.
The poor and the outcast
God's wounded, you'll see
Will wind up welcomed
By Jesus and me."

"Zacchaeus", says Jesus
with arms all around,
"Once you were lost
But now you are found."

First Frost

LUKE 17:11-19

Standing around and not under
Standing around and not up
Standing around and not by
Standing but searching,
Probing, testing,
You tease me
You tempt me
You tickle me
Tag! You're it!
Or am I?
Who's hiding?
Who's seeking?

Fact or fiction?
Figment of the imagination?
Filament of feeling?
Fragment of faith?
Some speak factually
God is....
Some speak fictively
God isn't....
Some do not dare to speak
but know You hide and seek

Standing around and not
understanding and not
upstanding and not
by standing but seeking You,
even if the evidence
is circumstantial.

Are these circumstances
glimmers of grace?
Hints of holiness?
Are they more than figments,
fragments, filaments,
conducing us to You,
used to us?
Was it a figment of my imagination,
a fragment of faith,
a filament of feeling,
or was the first frost
Your morning manifest?
Oh! all those frosted flakes,
fractals formed,
designs divined,
sunlight streaming
through windowpane?
Divine designs standing out,
outstanding to someone
standing around
seeking You in circumstantial
Evidence.

Worth the Wave?
Luke 18:35-43

Surf's
Building, breaking,
Cresting, crashing,
Tumbling, tunneling,
Whipping, wiping
Out to sea
Surfers
Wave watching,
Waiting, whiling away time
While whetting wants
For waves
Wet-suited
They wait
Not bored
But board
Climbing
a-board
Catching
a-wave
Riding
a-crest
Dreaming
a pipe
Then,
Crash, tumble
Wipe out!!!!
Crying, Christ!
Are you the surf
Or the surfer?
The wave
Or the waiver?
The dream
Or the dreamer?
The seen
Or the seer?

INRI
Feast of Christ the King

INRI
Four letters
Etched in wood
Ecce lignum
Behold the wood
Ide xylo
Eye the wood
What would I not do for you?
What wood we behold,
Jesu, Iēsous, Yeshua, held
from creche to cross.
Ecce lignum
Ide xylo
Behold the wood
Behold the babe
held by wood
How held?
In a manger
made of wood
What would he not be for you?

Ecce lignum
Behold the wood
Behold the boy
Jesu, Iēsous, Yeshua
The carpenter's son
wood-working
hands holding
hammer and nails
and sycamore

wood from trees
once grown, now hewn,
felled and feeling,
xylophonic.
What would he not be for you?

Ecce homo!
Etched in flesh
Behold the man
Ide Anthropos
Eye the human being
Divinely sent
on a fishing expedition
criss crossing Kinnareth
in wooden vessels
earthen vessels
holding fisherfolk.
Jesu, Iēsous, Yeshua
Miracle making
Sin absolving
Illness easing
Kingdom preaching
Bread taking
Wine blessing
Could cup and plate
made of wood
hold body and blood?
What would he not be for you?

Ecce lignum crucis
Ide xylo staurou
Behold the wood of the cross
Holding him,
Jesu, Iēsous, Yeshua
hammer and nails
and who knows
what kind of wood?
Christ's-crossing
Christ's-crying
Eloi! Eloi!
What would I not do for you?

WINTER
Quiver 2

On "That" Day
First Sunday of Advent
CYCLE A

Advent-sure as the day's dawning,
the sun's yawning,
rays reaching,
like arms in a morning stretch,
waking "this" day.
"That" day will have its say.
Advent-sure
is a hyphenated time,
linking past- present-
future, tense,
already - not yet,
then - now - then
time's over- over time,
still time - time still
a cosmic chiasm,
ABBA chiming
"That" day will have its say.
.
An alarm sounds!
Storm's soundings,
Winds wailing,
Whining, whistling,
Wake from sleep!
Is "this" "that" day?
Apocalypse nowadays
Noah-days
Crashing, thrashing
Waves washing over
Walls crumbling,
Tumbling down.
"This" day will have its say.

They say the Son came
once up on time.
Time's nodding, "Yes."
Time's knowing,
Now, comes the Son
"this" stormy sea-saw day
already - not yet
"That" day still has its say.

Advent- sure is an adventure!
See-saw
Past-present
Presence-passed
Now you see him —
Now you don't —
Heaven's hyphen
All in God's time
We know not
The day nor the hour
Only Now we know
To ask ABBA to give us
"This" day
While we while away the hours
Waiting for
"That" day.

On "This" Day

Advent —sure as "this" day's dawning,
the snows falling,
flakes flying,
like stars bursting in the eye
waking to white
"This" day will have its way,
a great white, broad way.
No need for neon.
Snow's show enough!
Light enough
to see by.
Silent enough
to hear by
Soft enough
to melt your heart.

In "this" snow light
In "this" silence
In "this" softness
you hear,
"Will you walk this way
with me "this" day?"
"Snow way," you say?
God's knowing you will
walk the snow-covered way
of the cross
No easy trek
trudging but not grudging
"this" wooded walk
branches bending,
weighed down
limbs leaning,
arched up and over.
Now a narrow way to walk.
an arrow points the way.
He leads, you follow
stopping by woods along the way,
"this" frosty day.

Way-stations
Rest stops for the weary.
Way-stations
Now shrouded in snow
Way-stations
Paths-crossing
Christ's life and
yours yoking
light as the falling
snow.

Oh the "thisness"
of an advent snowfall!
Oh, the haecceity
of "this" snow-struck day!
How could such suffering
Find its way to snowy woods
If it were not for "this"
labor of love?

The Baptist's Breach
Advent 2020

Howling, harrowing, hammering,
Havoc wreaking wind!
Wailing, whistling, whining,
Whorl- whirling wind!
Blustering, blistering, blasting,
Blowing bellows-like wind!
Herald-like, your voice
Shatters the silence.
Baptist-like, your power
Churns, turns
Serene seas to stormy.
Seizing the seas
Seizing the day!
A voice cries out of the wildness,
Prepare the waterways
weigh the weight
of sin and saving
grace, amazing
as it is.
One is on the way
Water walker
Water worker
Wonder worker
Heralding healing,
Forging forgiveness,
Repairing rifts,
Preparing gifts,
A table, tabula rasa,
Erasing errors,
Raising cain and

Able to calm and comfort,
Broken, bruised and beating the
Odds and even bettering the score
Against sin and death.
His love handles you with
tenderness.
Someone to hold on to.

What are you waiting for?
Take the plunge
Do the dive
Down, down
Comfort comes
in his embrace
and outstretched arms.
Comfort, the mantle,
the cloak he wears.
The calm will come
when you, crestfallen,
least expect
And crest rising
Christ rising
You'll ride the waves
With him;
Preparing the day
Savoring "this" day.

Gobsmacked
Wednesday of the Second Week of Advent
Isaiah 40:25-31 / Matthew 11:28-30

Winter's wearing
A white coat this morning
Physician for a weary,
Worn and sad soul.
Fusing hope and healing
Yoking love and longing
Joining joy with comfort
Winter's white coat
Wakes something within
Buried beneath life's burdens
Wary of trust, weary of time
Taking its toll.
White-coated winter
says,
"Open-wide,
say, Ahh"
"Aah, Aye!"
I'm gobsmacked
Wide-eyed
Agape
A gasp of wonder!
Such snow-white beauty!
Comfort, Yes!
Cold? No!
Warmth, Aye!
Snow melting
Something within.

God's wearing
A white coat this morning
A Dear and Glorious
Physician
Hope and healing fuses
Love and longing yokes
Joy and comfort joins
says,
"Open-wide,
say, Ahh"
"Aah, Aye!"
I'm God-smacked
Eagle-eyed
AGAPE
A gasp of wonder!
Such soaring spirit!
Growing young with
Heart, soul, mind and
Strength renewed.

Mary's Mind

1/1/2020

Another year's
"Here we go again"
Last year's
gains and losses
now seen in hindsight.
How does a hind see?
Deerly, watching,
still, frozen in time,
not knowing what's out there.
Hindsight is 20/20,
seeing clearly what was
is now but never shall be.
Now, and then,
a trigger!
She hies on hind legs
running, streams,
time ticking,
overtaking, fleeing.
A leap and crash!
A collision's cost
And all is lost.
Who knows what's
behind the seens?
Hindsight is 20/20.
Past yes, future no.

With hindsight
Would she have let him go?
Looking back
seeing what she has seen
knowing what she knows now
would she have let him leave?
Her past pondering
Her heart treasuring
Her once upon a time
Wondering what would be
Now knowing
What pain! what gain!
All would be lost
had she held on to him.
Had she a crystal bell
to tell the future
ringing in her ears,
hearing Hosannas
and cries of crucify
would her "let it be"
let her be?

Ah! men and women
wonder what will be in 2020?
What gains? What pains?
Oh! to have Mary's mind!
Fullness of grace
overflowing
not knowing
yet yearning
longing for love
made flesh in her.
Unsure,
yet surely accepting
what was, is now and ever will be.
Her hindsight is foresight
Believing and not seeing
with 20/20 vision.

2020's here.
Out with the old
In with the new
The ins and outs
The ups and downs
The dreams and doubts
The pains and gains
When will we ever learn?
When will hindsight
give us 20/20 vision
for the future?
As a deer longs for running streams,
humankind yearns for kindness
singing in perfect harmony
signing peace-abled treaties
treating the other as no other than
Oneself.
With hindsight
humankind should be more kind!
Oh! to see clearly to what we are called!
Oh! to see clearly into Mary's mind!
Oh! to see clearly what was and now what can be!
Hindsight in 2020?

Announcements
Baptism of the Lord

An ounce
meant to measure
volume or weight,
Wait, do tell
what difference
an ounce makes.
An ounce,
so small, slightly
more than a spoonful yet
much, much more than a mustard seed.
If you had an ounce of faith,
weigh what you might say.
words worth their weight in
gold, frankincense and mirth.
See, hear! Not hearsay, no,
Announcements!
Angel choirs caroling
Shepherd fears fleeing
Star's wonder
Magi wander
And
An ounce of faith becomes
a river
becomes a Baptist
announcing
a kingdom's dawning.

Undaunted, He comes
daring to descend
into the water,
opening the floodgates
Jordan's water breaking,
birthing, breaching
dolphin like, rising up for air.
Out and up and not away but with
Heavens helping
Dove davening
Voice announcing
"See, hear, the beloved."
Sun shining, shimmering
Glimmering, Gold now
Frankincense and Myrrh
will have its say another day.

Are you all here?
Hearers, no doubt?
Only an ounce of faith?
No need to turn up the volume.
A whisper,
A still, small voice
An ounce meant
To be enough.

Mind Meld

Mark 1:16-20

Keep mending
not minding
the one milling
about the shore
watching us
working our trade.
Our nets worth
wages and daily bread.
We must be about
our father's business.

John the younger
        jostles James
                the elder
Listen!
        His voice across the waters
My mind
        melding with his.
Mending me?
        Am I my net worth?
Listen!
        He's speaking to us
Trade trades,
        Fish for folk,
                Come after me,
                        Be the nets,
                              Untie the knots,
                                      Help them go free,
                                              with Me.

Zebedees do
jump ship,
cast themselves into
deeper waters
trusting the One
who melds minds
mends hearts
molds lives
to Him.

Ask Me? Ask You?

1 Samuel 15:16-23 / Mark 2:18-22

Ask and you shall receive?
Answers often deceive.
If I ask will I receive
a straight answer
or a crooked one
like the lines
that you right wrongs with?
Dare I ask you?
Why's the world askew?
From big bang to now
so much noise
alarums, alarms of war.
Both sides spoiling
a gag order from you.
"Wipe them out!
Wipe their slate clean!"
No more Amalekites flying
their banners of war
and Saul, salted with wounds
of war, spoiled no more.
Why's the world askew?
Because of you?
Do we put words in your mouth
and ideas in your head?
Your thoughts are not ours
for the taking or talking.

Dare I ask you?
Why's the world askew?
Even today the wrongs are
seen as rights.
Rants, raves, rallies
for guns and glory Hallelujah!
a God-given right to
carry arms and crush the enemy.
Aren't arms meant to carry
New-borns and old bones
To embrace and hold hands?
Aren't arms meant for shoulders
in solidarity, overcoming
differences and distances?
Shall we?

Even today we remember
A Dream so far
ahead of our time
words ringing
resounding, reverberating
words worth their salt
for a wounded nation.
Dream of chasms no more,
spasms of hate, no more
now hewn out of the mountain
of despair.
Hope's touchstone.
an MLK flying
high above and beyond
what dreams are made of.

Dare I ask you?
Why's the world askew?
Even today rights are
seen as wrongs by some.
Even today when we remember
an MLK dream,
rants, raves and rallies
hold sway,
far gone for guns.
A foregone conclusion?
A biased opinion?
Dare I ask you?
Is life a game of skins and shirts
breaking fast and furious
zig-zagging, skewed one way,
then the other
a full court press,
till one side wins?

Whine not!
You have the bridegroom
Christ's courting you
His skin, your kin
He's new wine for the old
world bursting at its seams
His new cloak clothing the
Tattered and torn fabric of
Life's hopes and dreams.

What a Whirl!
2 Samuel 6:12-23

Ark advancing
El Shaddai,
Shy, yet asking
Shall we waltz,
King?
or two-step
or tango
or try a tarantella?

Shall we dance,
King?
And I, David
answer with
abandon,
Ah! Yes! Today
shall be our
dancing day!

David dancing,
whirling, dervish-like
bowing, bending,
arc-like
arms akimbo,
swinging, swirling
swaying in ecstasy,
entranced.
Suffice it to say,
Shamelessly.

David dancing
A warrior waltzing
A leader leaping
A Kingpin spinning,
twisting, turning,
casting care to the wind,
carried away,
clad only in ephod,
baring his body and soul
to the whirl, for all to see.
Suffice it to say,
seamlessly.

Watching from a window
Michal sees and scorns
the dancer and the dance.
She cries and crows,
How humiliating!
How undignified!
Your kingly bearing betrayed,
barely clad, cavorting,
leaping like a gazelle,
A dancing King disgraced!
Suffice it to say
shamefully!

David divining
son Solomon's song,
"My lover leaps gazelle-like."
David rejoining
"Praise God in the festive dance!"
David rejoicing
"with timbrel and dance"
Suffice it to say,
What a Whirl!

Quite a Day!
02/02/2020

Luke 2:22-40

Feast of the Presentation

Quite a day for some
celebrating a Super
Sunday, today
or should we say
Two day?
or Too today
or tutu day?
It is, after all
02–02–20–20
A Palindrome,
forward and back
the same.
Like a game of football
which side will win?
Will one leave their heart
between a rock and
a hard place
and the other,
chiefly speaking
find everything up
to date on 02–02–20–20?
Oh, this is too, too much!
And it's not even a Tuesday!
Are the ground hogs
wearing tutus
as they search for a shadow?

A quiet day for some
celebrating a superb
Sunday, today
or should we say
a two day as well?
Two turtledoves
Two pigeons
Two parents
Two seers
Oh, say can you see
one light, one love
dawning for all.
A light casting shadows
causing contradictions
soul piercing
heart breaking
Love's palindrome.
Forward and backward
the same
Instant replay
from womb to tomb.
All in One life, One Love
On this Two day.

Quite a day for some
summing up thirty days of quiet,
presenting themselves each day.
Sitting in silence
holy ground hugging
between Brace rock
And a heart place.
Trusting the wisdom of elders.
Anna and Simeon say,
"Pray this way.
Tell-tale signs
wonders await you."
Christ's light illuminating
life's contradictions
life's Instant replays
up to this day and date.
Simeon like,
You break your silence
"Give him to me,
Give me Jesus"
Anna nods knowingly,
"Take and receive him.
Present him to the world.
Find him your All in All,
One life, One Love."

All this today?
02-02-20-20

Rendez-Vue

1 Kings 11:29-32 / Mark 7:31-37

Is a render one who rends?
A sender sends
A mender mends
A doer does.
A lover loves
But does a render rend?
Er… no,
If there were logic in language
or life for that matter,
one who rends a garment,
Ahijah-like,
would be a render.
but, no, a render
is a coat of many colored
paint or plaster
and to render
is to hand over.
Ah!Jah! I have it!
The cloak strikes twelve!
He rends the coat
and renders judgment
Jeroboam 10
Solomon 2
settling the score.

Sound resounds!
A heart rent in two!
Sound resounds!
Eph pha-tha!
No sound barrier now!
The Word
rendered.
The Word
heard
The silence rent in two
for one
for whom no sounds
resound till now.
An artist's rendering
Finger-pointing
Saliva saving
Ears opening
Tears tugging
at heartstrings
rending them
Speechless!
Loosing Love's tongue
Setting Love's score.

Sea Here

JAMES 1:1-11

See here!
James epistolizes.
Pistols drawn,
he shoots down
whoever wavers
warning,
"Doubt belies belief."
Whoever doubts
is like a wave
driven by the wind
tossed by the sea

See here!
It's a toss-up!
Belief or Doubt?
Heads or Tails?
Either/Or
Either way
It's easy to lose one's moorings
when wondering whether
all is chance or providence.
It's easy to lose one's moorings
when sleepwalking on water.

Sea Here!
I epistolize,
Pistils drawn
I seed belief.
In seas so serene.
one wonders,
"Where's the waves?"
I don't doubt
one could sleepwalk on water,
when seas awaken belief,
when faith flowers like
lily-pads and seals flip-flop
on sun-streaked rocks.

See Here!
James epistolizes.
He shouts down
doubters,
waving them off,
as unseaworthy vessels.
Am I one of them?
I do doubt
I don't doubt
I double up on doubt
When fierce waves awaken fears
Today's toss up?
Seeing seas so calm,
there is no need to flip-flop.
Belief is the winner.

Cristal–Eyes
Mark 6:30-34

Brisk and bracing,
a crystal-clear day dawning,
bright blue skies,
sun light shimmering
navy blue seas,
high now, low later,
morning's initiative.
An invitation to come and be
Caring's curator
Healed and healer
Sealed and sealer
Weal and welder

Heart's risk and racing,
no crystal clear, here hope's drowning
blood-shot skies
sunlight shivering
whine-dark seas
low now, always ebbing
and still —
Be still, my heart!
Christ's initiative
An invitation to come and be
Healed by the Healer
Sealed by the Sealer
Weal with the welder
A wider yoke for two

What medicine wheel
you take to heal
when pain drains
the life from you
the love from you?
A question mark?
or exclamation point!
You're the curator.
Will you choose
Christ's crystal?
The difference between
morning and mourning?
One and only U!

SPRING
Quiver 3

Lent/Easter
2020

The following poems were written just as the Covid 19 crisis was beginning to extend its reach into countries around the world. Soon the whole world would be in "lockdown."

What a Whorl!
Ash Wednesday

What a whorl we live in!
    Is life a line straight?
        An arrow from here to there?
Not on your life!
    No, life's eddy finding
        twisting, turning
            swirling, whirling
                storm's imprinting
            pooling and pulling
        this way and that
    and always whipping up
a fury and frenzy.
        Virile or viral?
            Our human weakness
                all at once in a whorl.

    Yes! Today
    a straight path
    from ashes to Easter.
(By the time we get to Phoenix,
    He'll be rising.)
    Even ashes etched
    in straight line
    cross-roads,
as if the journey would have
    clear markings!
    No, look closely!
    Ashes bear the whorls
    Of human fingers
    Imprinted on brows,
    beating the odds
of death's victory over life.

What whorl we do
    when ways are not straight and
        one strays, skipping along
            life's yellow trick road
                with its mindless,
                      heartless and cowardly
                            lines?

        "Choose life"
        Moses remans.
          "Lose life"
        Jesus reminds.
   If the world we live in
   were not such a whorl
   of choosing and losing,
  perhaps the path would
   be straight as an arrow
    from here to there
   from ashes to Easter.
At least this whorl we live
 bears the marks of him
 who imprinted his life
     on this world.
      Thumbs up!

Squirrel Scramble

ISAIAH 58:1-9 / MARK 9:14-15

I saw a squirrel
squatting on a stone wall
holding fast for a few seconds.
I wondered if he were feasting his eyes
on the golden kernel of sunrise
as I was
or was he in search of kernels of another kind?
Was he aching for acorns,
or fasting from feasting?
Was he searching for stores,
or asking for more
than oaks can provide?
"Squirrels do not live on acorns alone."

I saw a squirrel
Scurrying away
Holding fast no more.
Had his hunger tempted him
To break/fast from this glorious feast for the eyes,
this golden kernel of sunrise?
Had his aching for acorns
consumed him?
Has his searching for sturdy oaks
blurred his vision of sun's rising
over a rock of ages,
symbol of steadfast love?

                                          I saw myself in a squirrel
                                          scampering away from steadfast
                                          Rock and
                                          squirrel fortifying me
                                          with wisdom's kernels.
                                          Fast, yes, when it comes to acorns
                                          Fast, no, when it's time for slow.
                                          Hold fast to the one who
                                          Holds you
                                          Fast!

The Band Played On

It began with a band.
A strip of light elastic
Stretching horizon's length
A string of light fantastic
Separating sky from sea
And at the sight,
My heart beating
Drum-like
Rat-a-tat. Rat-a-tat

The band played on.
Measure for measure
More and more
Color's crescendo
Splaying across sky
Playing "on the sea"
Rubato reds
Obligato oranges
Jazzy blues and stretto yellows.
And at the sight
My heart thumping
Tuba-like
Oom-pah, Oom-pah

The band played on
Brash and brassy
A celestial organ sounding,
No muted trumpets or tones.
Bands of angels,
All coloraturas cry,
Pull out all the stops!
Let heaven display
Its power and its glory!
Holy, Holy, Holy,
Seraphim seen not heard
And at the sight,
my heart thrumming
strung like a band of light
across horizon's length
God's vibrato
Playing on my heartstrings.

Wicked Good!

Ezekiel 18:21-28

Wicked Good!
    Wicked which?
        Wicked evil, yes
            Wicked good, no
                One cannot be both/and
                      Or can one be two at once?
Wicked comes from wicca,
    Witch or wizard.
        Wicca which?
            One who casts spells
                And instills fears?
                    Or one who casts cares
                      To the west wind
                          Knowing nature heals,
                          Herbs powers
                      Nature's wizardry
              Drying herbs releasing
            Healing remedies.

Ezekiel assays,
Good as gold or
Wicked as a western witch?
Which is which?
Do not be so wick to judge,
Ezekiel essays to say,
"One's wick can absorb both
Good and evil
What makes the difference
Is what one does
Not 'who one is."
Will your wick work
For good and not for evil,
Burning brightly,
God's glow, sheen
And shine, waxing
And not waning?

Jesus, the wizard of us
Cast out demons and nets
Freeing some, catching others.
Jesus, the wizard of us
Knew how to cast spells
Knowing nature's healing.
A single word enough to hear
And be healed.
God was this wizard's
Source, sirree,
He sees the good as gold
In each and every
which way, he knows us
for what we are,
a patchwork of guilt and grace
a wick's work of guile and good
The wizard of Us knows we are
Wicked Good!

A Deer's Cry – In Hindsight

What does the hind see
as she wends her way
woods-wise,
stream searching,
suddenly stopping
sensing something
amiss?
Her eyes darting,
daring to look
left, right, before,
behind.
her neck craning,
tortuously,
she hides herself,
her hide standing on end
frozen in fear
blending in with
brush and bramble.
Time passes
Tick-tock
And still, motionless,
longing for running streams,
thirsting for living waters.

I remember a deer,
hind or hart
I don't remember.
Had it been a hart,
antlers may have been
antennas warning him of danger.

I saw the hind/hart running,
riveting my attention.
A lord-a-leaping!
A lady- dancing!
Nature's beauty bounding
over the marsh and main.
My heart beating and bouncing
with every leap and soar of this
hart unbound, hind unbidden,
coming out of nowhere.
And then, the crash,
unseen by eye, but ear shattering.
The heart-breaking collision.
Oh! my dear hart!
In hindsight,
I wish I could have warned
you of the oncoming calamity!
Would that you knew the "whys"
of your boundless bounding!
Were you longing for running streams?
Were you thirsting for living waters?

My dears cry these days,
calling out from quarantine,
cancelling dates and closing churches.
You, my dears, frozen in fear,
trapped in a blind of your own making,
Have you lost sight of me?
I have not lost sight of you.
I am the longing within you.
I am the living water
still streaming,
live,
still streaming
love.

Stag Leap
John 11:1-45

If the world were not the way it is
these days, this day
I'd gladly sing Your praise.

Watching waves washing white
foam forming frothing
peaked cap sizing
playful sea, I see.
How can this be, when the world is
ill, bedeviled by disease and despair?
Once upon a time they say you cast out
demons, bursting Beelzebul's bubble.
Can you not cast out this demon?
How many pleas and thanks do
you need before your heart is moved
to pity for this world, before you weep
as you did for your friend, Lazarus?
And as it was then, so it is now.
There is a stench that fills the air
that must be masked.
Disease, death and decay
are always that way
and the weary, wary world
wonders why and where and how
are you?

If the world were not as ill as it is
these days, this day
I'd easily sing Your praise.

Seeing sky's scrimshaw,
clouds crowding sun,
a light curtain alighting,
a mischievous morning,
my heart leaps like a stag,
trusting Christ,
stag like,
death destroying,
casting out demons,
but while we wait for his
Eastering, stone rolling, unbinding.
we must go stag.

Free for All
Palm Sunday
2020

Another Holy Week.
One like no other.
2020 vision's
blurred, bleary-eyed
scanning screens,
pads, phones. falderol.
Free-for-all
in turbulent times.
2020 vision's
clouded, cataracted
free falls,
tears and tears the
fabric of life.

An "other" Holy Week
past, presents
2020 hindsight.
Last years ago?
Looking back,
remembering
Hosanna shouts
Palms waving
People processing
Passion proclaimed
Bread broken
Wine poured
Touching hands and hearts
Ritual fare and fair
Play for us
Who have recourse to You.

An "other" Holy Week
Now no Hosanna shoutouts
but shut ins, all.
Now no palms waving or
woven crosses but
waving from a distance,
with palms washed.
Now no processions down aisles
but isolated one from another
No Passion proclaimed
but now live, lived, livid.
(Purple is Passion's color!)
Now no bread and wine
but bodies broken
And wine changed into watery tears
"Sunt lacrimae rerum"
Rare, yes,
once in a lifetime, one hopes,
tears for lives torn
Now no hands touch
but hearts, yes.
Now no ritual
except hand washing
Pilate wise
Now no Pilot but Christ
in his Passion.

Another Holy Week
One like no other
2020 vision
Far and near sighted
care filled, clear-eyed
from scanning
Hope's horizon
2020's vision
crowded, contracted
cross-eyed
One Love.
Free for All.

God's Free Day
Good Friday 2020

I should have shunned this morning's sunrise,
shouting
"Go back where you came from!"
What right have you to rise
shedding light rays cross sea and sky?
You should be shedding tears instead"
Who does Sun think he is?
Doesn't he remember the day when he refused to shine?
Wasn't he there when the world was shrouded in darkness?
Sun should be ashamed of shining this day!
Moon knows who she is.
Sun's glare of day is spared at night.
Moon masks our mourning.
She gives us just enough light
to carry on in this carrion time.

It was then as it is now
Then
The Word's flesh and blood
in the cross hairs of death and life
Now
the world's flesh and blood
in the cross hairs of contagion
Then
A grave for one, a grief for some
stabat mater, stoic John,
faithful women, flighty men
petrified Peter.

Now
Graves for many, a grief for all,
a world awash in tears.
The moon is more in tune with tears
than sun, basking in bravado.

I should have shunned sun's shining,
but, no, I could not turn away
even on this Good Friday.
It was stunning, you see,
as every day when it dares to rise and remind us
of another Rising
against all odds and even
in this carrion time
to carry on
in hope and not despair
and here and now
hear voices of the past,
those witnesses of
death's defeat and life's victory
calling today
God's Free Day.

DNA
Easter Sunday

I Dare Not Ask
if You are "truly" Risen as You said.
The question belies belief.
But how believe when all are stranded now
all islands, worlds
apart?
A parting is simply sorrow
Not sweet at all.

I Dare Not Ask
if You are "truly" Risen
when graves are all too common,
All for one and one for all
loved ones, side-lined
stranded
hearts
apart.

Am I gravely mistaken
or is there evidence
to the contrary?
If a single strand of hair
can tell a tale of who
and how and where
we've come from,
can we find a strand of here and now,
double helix of hope and healing
that tells the tale of who
and how and where
You've come from and are now?

I Dare Not Ask
The "how" of your rising.
The "who" and "why" we know.
A strand of Love, double helix
Jacob's ladder, ascending and descending,
Jesus' Spiral,
turning and returning.

I Dare Not Assume
A "Happy" Easter
when strands of sorrow
stretch a Cross
the world's horizon.
Would Hope/y Easter
serve us better,
be the leaven,
the light at the end of the tunnel?
A peek of sun
A peep of Alleluia
Belief in Your rising
Is in my DNA.

Twinning
2nd Sunday of Easter
Marathon Day 2020

"Spring is here," they say
but you could fool me.
This day chills to the bones
like the daily news that is not
new, nor good.
This bone-chilling cold and rain
says "stay inside," not out of doors,
locked for fear of life,
confined for dear life.
Where's hope behind closed doors?
This soul-chilling day makes one
recoil from Spring's promises
recalling what once was
upon a Springtime
flowers flourishing
trees re-leaving
people parading
lining streets with cheer and
cheers for chariots of fire,
those marathon marvels,
wheeling or self-propelling
towards the finish line.
Such wealth, common in Spring's time!
Recalling what once was.
recoiling from what now is I ask,
"Is this a marathon we're running?"
Now a new Heartbreak Hill
where countless numbers climb,
short of breath, side-pierced

with stitches, not the laughing kind and
winding up with wounds,
wound and bound, hands and feet
wondering where's the finish line
and crossing it
alone.

"Easter is here," they say,
but you could fool me.
This Easter chills to the bones
like the daily news that is not
good nor new.
These cold-shouldered days
turn one's insides out,
when lock up replaces
look up and out,
when there is no tender
to the touch.
Where's joy behind closed doors?

"Christ was here," they say
but you can't fool me
This upper room chills me to the bones
Like a spring fall of snow,
not due till winter.
Had Christ appeared to them
would there not be room for
warmth and cheer and toasting
and touching?
And looking out from this lock up,
wouldn't streets be lined
with crowds cheering on
life's long-distance runner?
Better doubt than disappointment.

"I Am, here," He says
And you can't fool me.
Your wounds are mine,
wound together as we are
bound as one body, we are
My tender is love for you
and this wounded world.
Unless I touch your wounds,
you will not believe.
Show me your hands.
They fit like a glove in mine.
Show me your feet
and walk with me.
(No need to keep your distance.)
Show me your side pierced
with pain's cutting edge.
Don't turn aside,
let me tender you
belief
and we'll finish the cross
aligned,
together.

Had
Third Sunday of Easter
Emmaus

Have we been "had,"
taken for a ride, sold a bill of goods?
Wouldn't a good God be better than this,
besting disease and death?
How many days is it now?
We've lost count.
Countless lives lost
counting for more
and not less
and still the daze
drag on,
this dragon slaying
life's good and better and best.
We "had" hoped
but hope now is as empty
as a tomb
a grave
six feet deep
distancing
love's embrace
leaves embers
and remembers
what hope had been.

A stranger speaks,
One who is no stranger
to death and disease.
His "dei" counts for all.
"What "dei" is this," you say?
This is the "dei" the Lord has made
Rejoice and be glad!
He had been "had,"
taken for a ride on a foal,
for thirty pieces of silver sold.
Why this way?
Why cross-way, cross wise?
Wise prophets foretold
something like this "dei"
But none could predict
this "dei" like no other,
asking all from one
and no other.
This "Had" held him fast,
past, over at last
breath, perfect
in its surrender,
tender love
unseen, yet soon
to be seen.
God's "dei"
slaying death's
dragon
once and for all.

But this day,
how hope?
"In the blessing,"
You say
"In the breaking,"
You stay
"In the giving,"
Your "dei"
Now, of necessity,
bread becomes body,
embers remember,
fire-breathing life into
hope that "had" been,
has been,
is and
always will be.
This is the "dei" the
Lord has made!

Come Back
JOHN 14: 25-26

Come Back!
Past Be Present!
Cri de cœur!
Heart's decree
or plaintive plea?
Will Past be the Advocate,
pleading our case?
Past knows well
our free-wheeling,
comings and goings
here and there
and everywhere
within and without
worry.

We the plaintiffs
register complaint
against the Present
who has left us orphaned,
bereft,
bereaving Past's
pleasures,
simple as Pi,
an infinite number
of goings and comings
greetings and gatherings
crowding and crowning
a day's work and play.

Now, no free-wheeling.
Life's circumference is
six-feet,
all around and under
for sum,
diametrically opposed to
what was Past.

"I must recuse myself,"
Past replies.
"I must refuse to advocate for you.
My comeback is this:
Present is my Future.
We are bound together as one.
What is your Present now
will one day be part of me,
Present wounds wound with Past.
Memory will serve as sigh
as this time goes by
presenting itself in another light."

Present, silent, until now,
takes a stand.
"I have no advocate but time's
ebbing and flowing, tide-wise.
The tide, too, will turn.
There is no going back in time.
Life wields weal both ways,
Wealth and welt.
Gain and pain
Profit and loss
But "now" has its promise as well."
Wells of love unseen,
Spirit yields
letting go graces
as countless as Pi,
Love's circumference
always expanding,
never contracting,
diametrically opposed to death.
You are always in Love's wheelhouse
After all, He came back
To be with you
Always.

Cobble's Tones
Pentecost

Most mornings I cobble together
Bits and pieces of prayer
Words, phrases, verses,
 not averse to images.
 A startling sunrise
 Sunlight's reflection
  Refracting off surf's surfaces
   Looking like streets of cobblestone.
   An invitation to walk on water?
   Surely, I would sink, like Peter,
    That Rock of ages
    To ocean's floor
    The weight of my sins
     Dragging me down
     Drowning in despair.
      Each pebble, stone or rock
      On ocean's floor
       A memory of a cobblestoned life.
       And then the outstretched hand,
       Drawing me up and out and
       Speaking words of wisdom.
        Not fearing but faring well,
        Listening in the Son light
        And the cobb/gull
         Glistening in the sunlight.
                    Like ocean's floor
                   My prayer, the same,
                  Some rough patches
                 Summing up a patchwork of
                This memory and that hope
               That memory and this prayer.
              This word-cobbler means to mend minds
And melt hearts of stone.

Do the gifts of the Spirit
come from the Divine cobbler?
Kernels of wisdom,
knowledge,
understanding,
off the cob of Sofia
Her ear attuned to our need,
inspiring courage and counsel
instilling reverence and being still in
awe and wonder.
Take my words with a grain of salt,
if you will, but let Sofia's
be silken, soothing broken hearts
smoothing the way that wearies.
Who better to mend the soul
than the Divine Cobbler?

An Earful
(for Ann Harris Jacobs)

I wish I were gifted with a good ear!
If I were, I'd be attuned to hear
music's mystery more perfectly
pitched to catch
fourths and fifths
circling sounds
ringing tones
singing solfege
on key,
Oh me, oh my
ear is so ordinary
I can tell the difference
between harmony and discord
but no, not the intervals
that have me at sixths and sevenths.
Oh! for an octave! Do-si- do tell!
Tonic for an ill-equipped ear!

I wish I were gifted with a good ear!
If I were, I'd be attuned to hear
the breathless cries of protest
A fevered pitch, catching fire
despite curfew, care for a few?
Not even, just to spite,
a circle of fists, pummeling protest
tone deaf to timeless
crucifixion.

Oh me, oh my
ear is pierced
with sound stirring
gasps for air
No harmony hear
Just discord.
But then, a whispered voice,
Spirit's gift of good counsel,
An ear to hear God's song,
sung by People Up in arms
locked together in peaceful protest.
"What color is God's skin?"
the song ringing in ears,
beginning with mi, it scales down
and up again to find its rest in
Sol. Music to my ear.

SUMMER
Quiver 4

Soul-Stice

Jerimiah 20:10-13

Be still my soul!
Stop brooding over flaws, faults and failings,
missteps, faux pas, paths mis-taken,
foot falls and fault lines.
Falling afoul in death traps,
the fowler snares, foul, not owl- wise
always, whispers of wrongs done,
your undoing,
transgression trapping you still.
Is there egress from past's failures,
a greener grass on the other side,
an escape cause for the unshriven soul?

Be still my soul!
Be brewing a love potion,
A double portion of mercy's minding, mending,
easy to swallow.
A brood of sparrows (more than two) be
soul's solace,
be an arrow piercing you with love's luster!
Be still my soul!
Still as the waters running deep within,
still as ocean's entrancing tranquility,
lapping quietly,
an infant's sleep in her mother's lap
a child asleep in his father's arms.
Still.

A Paean for Peonies
Trinity Sunday

I'd like to compose
a paean for peonies,
those posies who rival roses
not in perfume but in pomp,
pom-poms, cheering the eye
and heart of the beholder.
We should be beholden
to the Creator
for peonies' pomp and
Eye-popping Beauty.
Their circumstances remind us
of how we hope to be seen.
Their short-lived lives,
begin as perfect orbs,
self-contained,
holding their beauty
close to the vest,
meant for us to "ooh" and "ah"
as we wait for them
to show their raiment
in all its panoply.
They pop open,
bursting at the seems
like proud parents
of new-borns.
Peonies have no need
for self-promotion.
Their beauty is self-evident
a reflection of divine
Perichoresis,
A "peonies waltz"
In Trinity's time.

Clean Slate

Sky's slate of late.
There are no hues of blue,
no use for teal's truth telling,
tossing puff pillows,
cushioning the blow of
corona's contagion.
Grey's in play these days.
Sea's slate of late.
There are no hues of blue,
no use for turquoise's teasing,
tempting treasures,
hidden beneath.

Steel grey sea and sky?
Cold comfort for a world
weft and bereft
in time's warp,
a world turned outside in,
and downside up,
skating on thin ice,
slated for who knows what,
salted with tears for years
past, this present, tense
with worry and why?

Oh! for a blank slate!
for a world washed clean
of illness and disease
of isms of all kinds
of harrows of all kens.
Oh! for a clean slate!
for a world wiped clean
of sin and division,
by Love's erasures,
ensuring peace and polity.

Oh! for a state of grace!
for a Garden grown again
of Eden's memories,
free of weeds, thorns and thistles
that choke, hold, pierce and prickle,
In this garden grows the treat
of knowing only good, not evil.
The divine Gardener with wheel
barrow filled with our regrets,
now compost for composing
a kindom come.

Can I see in sky's slate and
sea's steel grey hue-less,
God's true blueness,
washing clean,
wiping clear,
emptying my barrow full of
weal and woe?
Can I find within my soul
a garden growing
Eden-like,
returning to innocence
Love's letting
Love's leaving
Love's lettering,
room and board for
new beginnings?

Soul's slated for
Christ's compassion.
Scarlet sins now
Alabaster white,
Soul's steel, once
Iron clad, now
Stainless, alloyed with
Christ love,
aligned with Christ's yoke.
A clean slate!

Full Grown

Romans 8:18-23 / Matthew 13:1-10

"How goes it?" You ask.
"So-so," I say.
"So, I see," You say.
"So, You know," I say.
What can you expect
when creation's groan
is deafening,
ear-splitting,
crying out for air
pods to stifle the sounds
of labor's pains,
pandemic's futility?
Yet Love's placenta,
providing promises,
transitioning,
birthing a new creation,
choosing to hear
soul soothing,
music to the ear
pulse and rhythm
reminding of more,
so much more
so much, much more
than mask and misery!

"How goes it?" I ask.
"Sow-Sow," You say.
"What's that?" I ask,
"You're only so-so?"
"No," you say, "SOW,
double you,
seen but not heard,
sewn but not grown.
My word still lies fallow
waiting for a birth
harrowing your soul,
transitioning to more
fertile than futile
and so, I'm rooting
for you."

"How goes it?" You ask.
"Sow-Sow", I say.
Is my soul rich enough
soil for the planting?
Will your roots reach
down, holding me fast,
tenacious! We'd
better be careful,
not carefree,
you and me.
Your harrowing
makes for hallowing.
What once was groan
is now full grown!

A New Brew
Matthew 13:24-30

Something's brewing!
A week's worth of work,
sowing scripture's seed,
tilling soul's soil
with His stories sewn with
yours, truly,
toiling in Eden's garden,
again, a time of innocence,
asking over and over,
to know and be known
to love and be loved
to simply serve or
better, serve "standard"
fare at love's banquet,
tempting one with tastes of
savory "meets" and sweet deserts,
"pears" of three kinds,
served with slices of
"humble" pie,
and colloquy's quaffs,
quenching soul's thirst.
S'mores to come.

Someone's stewing,
A weed's work is worth
sowing Satan's seeds
instilling soiled, soulless.
Doubt and distrust,
"Standard" fare for
Love's enemy,
Leviathan's leaven,
sewn serpentine,
entwining,
winding itself around
snaking its way up and down
stalking wheat.
With wheat and weeds
wound round,
who will win now?

Must one wait,
chafing at the bit,
until good grain
has its sway
and harvest day
is come again?
Or, even now,
know Love's Sovereign,
discerning spirits,
distilling ails and all
your true heart's
desires into a
new brew,
drinking from His cup?
Mean, wily Satan's
left to stew
in his own juices…

Undertow

Matthew 13:44-46

A mother's cry,
"J'avais perdu la foi."
Un cri de cœur.
"I have lost faith."
A mother's cry,
"I have lost my son!"
Priceless pearl more treasured than any faith
in heaven or on earth.
She, shell-shocked and no current
can revive her.
Her beloved son
ripped from her,
swept away,
Death's undertow taking him from her.
Her priceless pearl,
more treasured than any life.
Time and tide wait for no one.

She waited once,
wading in baptismal water,
knee deep in love's promise,
Santiago's shell scooping,
life-saving water streaming,
daring dreams of new life.
Christ's undertow
was pulling her beneath the water,
only to revive and find
the breath of new life,
a new heartbeat of
Love from the Risen One.

But now, she who once trusted,
feels faith's betrayal.
" I have lost faith" her cry.
Rivulets of tears streaming,
she, a shell that longs to hold again
her precious pearl,
now holds only the "remains of his days,"
an earthen vessel in her hands that once held
him new-born, on Assumption day.
Her heart, her hands, her soul
Empty. Vide.

A mother's cry
"I have lost my son."
Her pearl of great price,
promised by angel's whispers
her heart's treasure
filled with great promise,
casting nets, sounding calls
to come and follow.
Her heart now hollowed out
by Cross currents,
sweeping him away,
Death's undertow taking him from her.
Time and tide wait for no one.

She waited once,
wading into faith's deep waters.
Would the One who engendered life
within her womb now let her barren be?
Would tomb be Love's womb,
birthing Risen Life?
Her heart ruled in Yes's favor.
She, an empty shell, waiting to be filled
again, knowing, the tide would shift and change.
No undertow would be a match for the Maker.

Where once an angel's voice was heard in greeting, hailing her
now another's overheard
and under tow to Love's yoke,
"Mary," she hears, "Rabbouni,"
"Peace!" resounds in her ears.
"Give me something to eat!"
"I've heard him say that how many times?
Something to tide him over until the next supper! Come and have breakfast!
Where did he learn how to cook?"
She smiles a knowing smile,
Reaching through time to now
embrace Fatima, Maria and all who have lost a pearl of great price,
knowing faith will find them.

Days' Daze

Naham 2/3 / Matthew 16-24-28

This day's dawning
deserves a 5-star rating!
Razzle-dazzle reds,
Pinks and purples with pizzazz,
Bedazzling blues,
Huzzah for the hues!
One wakes from triple z's
to skies and seas of double z's,
puzzle pieces, seen
interlocking
jig-dancing.
All creation's a -buzz

These days do not
deserve a single star-
crossed, they are.
More daze than dazzle,
news not new
but day's old,
age-old love
fizzles as one daze
follows another.
Frizzled nerves now,
muzzled by masks, we
not knowing
what new puzzle awaits
with no solution.
A-cross and Down
We go.

That day, they say,
will merit more stars than
skies can bear.
Nahum knows no
hum drum,
ho hum,
doldrum daze,
but days dawning, sizzling hot,
a jazz improvisation on
age-old,
Love's
Interlocking
pieces
A dizzying paradox or puzzle?
How can loss be gain?
Caught in the Cross fire,
we zig and zag,
jig and jag,
wanting to wake
from Z's,
To why
and
You.

Be Still!

1 Kings 19:9-13 / Matthew 14:22-33

How be still
When world's woes
Whip all into a frenzy
Feeding fears of
Stark infested waters?
Cross winds,
World winds,
Wailing, while at the
Fourth watch he
Walks forth
Towards them.
Storm-tossed seas
Cannot seize the
One whose sigh
Summons silence.

But how be still
When virus's
Seismic show
Opens maw and maw
Swallows one up and
Drains down,
Into another abyss,
Where one quakes
And quivers,
Wondering if there will ever be
Solid ground to walk on?
While at the fourth watch
He walks forth
Towards us,

Closing the gap,
Fear's chasm now
Abridged.
Gaping maws of earth
Cannot consume the
One whose words
Command calm.

But how be still
When fire powers
Fear and frenzy,
And there is no port
In a storm and
All "rues" are rubble now,
Now no ruse,
No masks to hide behind?
Fear's here and now
Burns away hopes and
Dreams are swallowed up
In night maws,
Frightened by the ghosts
Of past wars and lost lives.
Will He watch
And walk with them?
Will fiery furnace
Consume the One
Whose body is broken
Whose blood is poured out
Whose spirit is the breath of life
For all?

Will the cacophony of
Sounds from
Whipping winds,
Quaking earth,
Flaming fire
Drown out the
Voice of the One
Who summons silence,
Commands calm,
And who "Still" speaks?

Duple Time
Jerimiah 20:7-9 / Matthew 16:21-27

"Double timer!"
"You duped me!"
Jeremiah's javelin,
Love deceived,
Spear meant to
Pierce the heart
Of the Lover
But boomerangs
Similar sentiments
"Return to sender"
Forth and back
Words fly
Sly as a fox
Trotting
Traps set
Tramping on
Tripping up
Weighed down
And whoosh!
The Divine Trapper
Ensnares his heart
Burning embers
Passion plumbs the
Debts of love
Offered and welcomed
For a time
Face to face
A dance in duple time.

God forbid!
No such thing!
Peter's hammer thrown
Words, cast like nets,
Yet missing the mark.
His harmatia?
Death denying!
Back and forth
Words fly,
Slinging shots,
Put to the test
His first denial
Portends another
In triple time.

Who duped you?
Satan's seduction?
Jesus's javelin,
Passion's pointed
Spear meant to
Pierce Peter,
Fool of himself.
"Get behind me!"
Back turned
no turning back
for Him
on the way,
weighed down
by cross and cruelty
a contretemps
a dance in duple time.

All's Fare
ISAIAH 25:6-10 / MATTHEW 22:1-14

Full Fare on the menu
for "that day."
God's banquet once
and for all
rich and juicy
meet and just
for all nations.
Wayfarers all,
once worlds apart
now wound together
winding their way
to "this" mountain.
Isaiah' sees and sings,
"Wholly, Wholly, Wholly
One for all and all for One"
It's fare enough
for all wayfarers,
more than enough
to feed the five thousand
and the more
the merrier
when wine flows freely
and all meet
as brothers and sisters.
What appeal there is
when food is more than fare
and well-being is not wanting!
It is meet and just!

Meager fare on the menu
for "these days."
Life's banquet once
with so many choices
now so few
and fare between what is
and once was.
Appetizers on the menu, yes,
but only eyed
not tasted,
whetting wants for
friendly feasts
grateful gatherings,
hope, holding hands
around tables of plenty.
Sparse and spare,
"Unfair," we feel
famished.
Food does not suffice
or drink quench thirst.
What serves rich food
and choice wine
when all must be at separate tables?
What appeal is there
when food is only fare
and well-being is left wanting?
It is not meet nor fair.

All's fare
in love and
wherever two are
gathered in more
than name only.
More fast than feast
these days,
a limited menu
but fare enough
to help us hunger
for the body of Christ
who is more than
bread and
why not note
the ways
You carry us
these pandemic days?
What appeal there is
when fare is more than food!
It is meet and just right!

Levi-Tation

His custom was to rise
early in the morn.
No night owl, he
but desert owl's hoot
would wake him from
dreamless sleep.
No dreamer, he,
when day's drudgery
awaited.
His custom table
would soon be
taxing his patience
with queues of the querulous
quarreling, questioning,
cursing him.
And he, accustomed to
their disgust and disdain,
would return insult with injury,
a counter, a tax-charged
sum for himself
to balance the scales
of their scorn.

Accustomed he was
to dreamless sleep
lest day's burdens
be night's as well
No rest for the weary,
yoked, as he was
to table and chair,
counting coins with
Caesar's countenance
until day's end.
But dream he did,
Joseph-wise one night.
A cloak of many colors,
custom made, he wore
the weave in dream's day.
A "magi-cal" mantle it was!

When worn,
a "seer" he becomes,
a star in the East he sees
"Hee-haw," he divines,
Balaam-like, now
His fortune told,
wrapped in this mantle of
prophetic voices,
mingled with Moses's
mountain ascending
desert crossing,
a face seen,
a voice heard,
"Come"
Command or invitation?
And then,
an owl's hooting
An Awakening!

His custom was to walk
a pace, quickening
his step, shunning
shouts of "Unclean"
shoulders cold,
avoiding the sinner
at all costs
This day, though,
he finds the tables
overturned
no money changing hands
someone is waiting,
a face seen
a voice heard,
once upon a dream.
His name heard,
His soul soars,
on eagle's wings.
He leaves his
Custom-Aerie
And he follows.

To Know A Veil

Not a line drawn in sand,
Whose crossing means
Risk and reckoning.
No, a sky-line
Straight across horizon's
Length, a line meant
For best and beckoning.
Can you divine
the divine
drafter's drawing you in?
Sky scanning,
Wondering whoziwhat's
Behind the curtain,
Sky searching
Reading the sighs of the times,
Waiting for the veil
To be lifted
But
To no avail.

And suddenly,
You see more of me,
The curtain rises
Revealing me,
A lonely figure
On this world's stage,
Longing for a role to play,
Available for the part
But my heart's
Unavailable, still.
Stealing the scene,
You hide behind the veil
And I watch and wait
For the unveiling....

What's Now?

What's now these days
when now is not new,
but old, bits and pieces of
what was once and
is not now?
We've been robbed
of now, and then
we sew patches of
past on time's cloak.
Threadbare, we,
weary and worn down.
Why sew?
How so?
When hopes and
dreams are tattered
and torn into pieces,
in this time
we call "now."

What's new these days
when new is not now
but auld, longing for
what was and waiting for
what will be, will be?
Ringing out the old,
bringing in the new,
Hope springs, sings,
wings its ways with
promises, more or less?

What now, while time
tempts a fuller future,
not this "now,"
shrinking in sighs,
shrunken to mostly
memories,
a distressed fabric?
How sew this "now"
"new" shrunken cloth
on auld lang time?
How to be or not to be
in this mean/time?

That is the question!
The answer heard
In voices past,
Hallowed be their names.
How sew, they say?
Walk the way
Be the blessing!
Not "now" robbed but
robed in white you are,
blessed are you, know it or not,
Spirit-rich and poor you are,
this mourning becomes you.
What's "now" and "new?"
That is, "so you!"
So be it!

Enthralled

In whose thrall are you held these dire days?
In fear's thrall, through it all?
We dare to call these days "dire"
when crises cast sufferings' shadows
cross worlds apart from one another.
"Dire" derives from "dirus,"
Fear incarnate,
the worst is yet to be
In fear's thrall,
a chain reaction
bound to come bust or Boom,
come Hell or high water.
Well, held in fear's fist,
A grip tight,
ropewalk taut,
A high wire,
strung out-
stretched arms,
crosswise.

In whose thrall are you held these dear days?
In Christ's thrall, through it all?
How dare we call these days "dear"
when one is filled with dread for dear ones
at great cost, deprived of one another?
"Dear" derives from "dier" and "duur"
"beloved" and "costly"
Double Dutch words
as twin ropes intertwined,
heart's skipping
the best is yet to be

In Christ's thrall,
An unchained reaction,
bound to come best and bloom
first and fruitful.
Weal, yes, and held in His grasp,
Crosswalk taught,
His high wire strung
A cross, the universe.
Love's gravitational pull
In this heart string theory.
Are you yet enthralled?

And How!
Feast of the Immaculate Conception

I woke to wonder
"How can this be?"
It wasn't foretold
as far I know.
White, light and
fluffy as Angel's wings,
this new fall
making all
immaculate
For now
no earth stains
visible to the eye.
The barren branches
with limbs akimbo
unkind reminders of death
and decay now
adorned in white,
looking to all the world
like a bride, waiting.
No grooming needed.
Let it be down to them!
Nature's immaculate
conception?

She woke to wonder
"How can this be?"
She knew the foretelling
from a far-off prophet's voice,
"Isaiah," she sighs "ah!"
"But how now?"
"Who, me?"
White, light and
winged wonder speaks,
"The ancient Fall
now new in you,
stainless, stealing
sin's scepter,
your scion,
this shoot from Jesse's
tree will wield love's power,
yet yield to cross and cruelty
death's reach now all akimbo.
And you, adorned in white
Looking to all the world
Like a bride, waiting.
No groom needed.
Let it be!
And how!

NOTES

To see the photo images that inspired many of these poems, go to
robertvereecke.org

All A Quiver
MARK 9:14-29

The first poem in this collection is dedicated to Jesuit poet Gerard Manley Hopkins. His love of language, rhythm, the "thisness" of each and every element of creation has been the major influence on my own poetic imagination. This poem was inspired by a morning walk on Cape Cod with GMH as my companion.

AUTUMN
Quiver 1

Going Poem Picking
This poem is dedicated to Mary Oliver and St Francis of Assisi, both very much in love with God's created world. Each experienced creation as an invitation into the mystery of the Creator. Her poetry and his praise are inexhaustible sources of light and delight. It was that experience of delight that I hoped to capture in this poem.

Over the Moon
This poem is also dedicated to Mary Oliver and St. Francis of Assisi. It was written on his feast day, October 4th, 2019. Its inspiration comes from his "Canticle of Praise."

Seas, the day!
A three-day Nor'easter off the Gloucester coast in October 2019 was the inspiration for this quartet of poems. The first three begin with the same chorus of words, sounds and syllables that try to capture this fierce storm. Echoing the sounds of the storm are the voices of Malachi, Joel and Elisha. The fourth poem is the calm after the storm.

Gully Gee!
When you live by the ocean and can witness the sun rising every morning, there can be a tendency to compare one day to another. This was a day I learned my lesson!

Tea for Two
Written for the feast of Teresa of Avila, mystic and Doctor of the Church, this poem imagines her having tea with the poet, Mary Oliver. I imagined they had a great deal to chat about.

Luke and See
Written for the feast of St. Luke, this poem plays with words as it tries to encapsulate his Gospel in five stanzas. The inspiration came from the first reading of the day from 2nd Timothy: *When you come, bring the cloak I left with Carpus in Troas, the papyrus rolls, and especially the parchments.*

The Prayer-We Breathe
LUKE 18:1-8

Working at a retreat house where prayer is our daily fare, I have been struck how one's prayer changes with the seasons. If we let creation teach us to pray, we can learn a great deal.

Cache or Credit?
LUKE 12:13-21

This is one of the poems that I hope is "catchy."

Autumn Weaves

Written for the feast of St Anthony Claret, this poem was inspired by the fact that his father was a weaver as was he for a brief time. The image of weaving is used throughout.

Autumn Belief

Written for the memorial of all the faithful departed, this poem invites the reader to see the leaves of autumn as a reminder of the brevity of our human lives and yet holding the promise of something more to come.

Aye, Aye!
ROMANS 8:18-25

I see the sea every day, and with my love of words sounding the same but having very different meanings, I couldn't resist writing this, especially with the scripture of the day being Romans 8!

Autumn's End
ROMANS 8:26-30

"Likewise, the Spirit helps us in our weakness; for we do not know how to pray as we ought, but the Spirit intercedes for us with sighs too deep for words." The poem tries to "flesh out" what it means to let the Spirit teach one how to pray.

More Prose than Cons
ROMANS 8:28

"We know that in everything God works for good with those who love him."

Really? When you have experienced trauma or tragic loss, do you believe that what you have gone through is for "good?" The key to the poem is the X in its variety of meanings.

Zach's Zounds
LUKE: 19:1-10

"Zounds" is a late 16th century exclamation that is a contraction of the words God and wounds. Unlike, most of the other poems in the collection, there is a consistent meter and rhyme scheme. I wanted it to sound like a modern day "rap."

First Frost
LUKE 17:11-19

"Stand up and go; your faith has saved you."
"In all circumstance, give thanks."

These words from the Gospel and the acclamation for Wednesday of the 32nd Sunday in Ordinary Time, combined with the first frost on the windows of the Mary Chapel at the retreat house, were the inspiration for this poem. The first four lines of the first stanza have two possible meanings, depending on whether the reader pauses at the end of each line or connects them with the next.

Worth the Wave
LUKE 18:35-43

If the surf's "up" in Brace Cove, one can see surfers waiting for a wave to ride. The blind beggar in this Gospel passage also waits, and when he knows who is passing by, he cries out, never dreaming of what Christ can do for him.

INRI
Feast of Christ the King
LUKE 23:38

"There was also an inscription over him, "This is the King of the Jews."

The Gospel of John tells us that the inscription was written in Hebrew, Latin and Greek. Hence the repetition of the name of Jesus in those languages. "Behold the wood of the cross" is sung three times during the liturgy of Good Friday. The Latin translation is "Ecce lignum crucis." The Greek is "Ide xylo stauro" (a xylophone originally was made of wood).

WINTER
Quiver 2

On "That" Day
The scriptures during the Advent season frequently begin with the words, "On that day," portending hope or cataclysm in the future. Advent is all about time. We remember the three "comings" of Christ; in past, present and future.

On "This" Day
An early snowfall in Advent cloaked the landscape with a mantle of white. The "Way of the Cross" was weighed down with snow; exquisitely beautiful but challenging to walk. The reference to "thisness" or "haecceity" comes from the Medieval Philosophy of Duns Scotus. Gerard Manley Hopkins was influenced by this school of thought.

The Baptist's Breach
This poem was written for the 2nd Sunday of Advent in 2020. It begins with the same measures as the Nor'easter poems of 2019.

Gobsmacked
Isaiah 40:25-31 / Matthew 11:28-30

Another snowfall left me "gobsmacked." The "white coat" that winter was wearing reminded me of a physician's white coat. Both readings of Wednesday of the 2nd Week of Advent are about healing, especially Jesus' invitation:
"Come to me all you who are weary and find are burdened, and I will give you rest."

Mary's Mind
1/1/20
When I wrote this poem on January 1st 2020, no one could have imagined what the year would bring. Since 20-20 is associated with vision and hindsight, this was the theme that is woven through the work. I also remembered seeing a deer making its way through the marshes in East Dennis, Cape Cod. There was such beauty and power in its stride and then as it leapt to cross the road it collided with a vehicle and was killed instantly. In one fleeting moment, all was lost for the poor deer.

The pandemic of 2020 makes this poem all the more poignant reading it on January 1st 2021.

Announcements
Baptism of the Lord
The Christmas Season comes to an end with the feast of the Baptism of Jesus. Throughout the season, there is one announcement after another; to the shepherds, the magi and the "voice from heaven" that announces, "This is my beloved Son."

Mind Meld
Mark :16-20
The call of James and John. Are they more than their nets' worth? Read and see!

Ask Me? Ask You?
1 Samuel 15:16-23 / Mark 2:18-20
The writing of this poem coincided with Martin Luther King Day and anti-gun control protests in Richmond, Virginia.

What a Whirl!
2 SAMUEL 6:12-23

As a choreographer interested in the integration of dance and religious expression, I have always thrilled to this passage of David's dancing before the Ark.

Quite a Day!
02/02/20/20

This was quite a day! A date with a palindrome of numbers. It was Super Sunday, (Kansas City Chiefs vs. San Francisco 49'ers). It was the feast of the Presentation and the final day for retreatants who had spent the last 30 days making the Spiritual Exercises of St Ignatius.

Rendez-Vue
1 KINGS 11 / MARK 7:31-37

The poem invites the reader to "look again" at these scriptures, which seem to have nothing in common but seen together can "render" a different conclusion.

Sea Here
JAMES 1:1-11

An obvious play on "sea" and "see." The calm sea here contrasts with James' stormy language regarding those who doubt and don't see.

Cristal-Eyes
MARK 6:30-34

"Come away by yourselves and rest a while." The poem is an invitation to see and know the compassion of Christ. It is an invitation to experience the healing power of Christ, like crystals that are used for healing.

SPRING
Quiver 3

What a Whorl!
Ash Wednesday

A "whorl" is a pattern of spirals or concentric circles. It's what distinguishes a fingerprint. It seemed an appropriate symbol for the ashes that are signed on one's forehead with the fingerprint of another.

Squirrel Scramble
ISAIAH 58:1-9 / MARK 9:14-15

Both of the scriptures for the Friday following Ash Wednesday speak of "fasting." Another word with many meanings!

The Band Played on

Although this poem was written in the first week of Lent, it is not connected with a particular scripture. It echoes the cry of the seraphim in Isaiah 6 but its inspiration comes from being "dazzled" by the predawn and sunrise.

Wicked Good
EZEKIEL 18:21-28

Written for Friday of the first week of Lent, this poem plays with the contemporary expression "wicked good!"

A Deer's Cry – In Hindsight

Written in the second Week of Lent, this is a companion poem to Mary's Mind. By this time the pandemic had paralyzed the world and "hindsight" had taken on a more poignant meaning.

Stag Leap

"The Raising of Lazarus," the suffering from the pandemic, the Eastern Point sea/sky and the promise of Easter are all woven together in this poem for the 5th Sunday of Lent.

Free for All
Palm Sunday 2020

God's Free Day
Good Friday 2020

DNA
Easter 2020

Holy Week 2020 was like none other we have experienced. Weaving together the events of this most sacred time with the inability to celebrate them liturgically because of the pandemic, these poems try to interpret the meaning of our "now" in the light of the "then."

Twinning
2nd Sunday of Easter

There was no Marathon Monday in Boston in 2020. It was the custom to watch the runners come from climbing "Heartbreak Hill" and running down Commonwealth Avenue to the finish line. "Twinning" weaves together the themes of Thomas, the Twin's doubt with the pandemic's power to make skeptics of us.

Had
3rd Sunday of Easter

The Greek word "dei" is central to the Lucan passage of the disciples on the road to Emmaus. It means "it had to be or it was necessary." "Dei" sounds like "day" and both have their "day/dei" in Had.

Come Back
JOHN 14:25-26

This poem written for Monday of the fifth Week of Easter uses the Johannine image of the Advocate. In "Come Back," the case is made against the Present asking the Past to plead our cause. It is the Spirit as Advocate who comes to our aid.

Cobble's Tones
Pentecost

At tines the reflection of the sun on the water looks like a cobblestone road that one could walk on. BTW, a "cobb" is a seagull!

An Ear Full

This poem is dedicated to Ann Harris Jacob, friend and gifted musician. It was written after the protests following the death of George Floyd.

SUMMER
Quiver 4

Soul-Stice
JERIMIAH 20:10-13

The word "solstice" literally means "sun stopped or still." Written for solstice day, June 21st, the poem is an invitation to let one's "soul" be "still."

A Pean for Peonies
Trinity Sunday

Peonies are one of the most beautiful summer flowers. The deserve a "paean" written for them!

Clean Slate

During the month of July at Eastern Point, retreatants come to make the 30-day Spiritual Exercises of St Ignatius. The first dynamic (week) of the Exercises is the invitation to come to know oneself as a sinner who is unconditionally loved by God.

Full Grown
Fifteenth Sunday in Ordinary Time

Romans 8:18-23 / Matthew 13:1-10

The seed for this poem was planted in the soil of the Parable of the Sower.

A New Brew

Matthew 13:24-30

In the second dynamic or "week" of the Spiritual Exercises, there is a meditation on what Ignatius calls The Two Standards, one being the Standard of Christ and the other that of Satan. There are also meditations on "Three Pairs of Men" and "Three Degrees of Humility," as well as instructions of "discernment of spirits." Using the Parable of the Weeds and the Wheat, the poem "harvests" all of these themes for those making the Spiritual Exercises.

Undertow

Matthew 13:44-66

Fatima Koné is a woman from the Côte D'Ivoire whom I baptized three years ago. At the time, she was filled with life and great fervor for her new found faith. Last year I received word that her 22 year old son had died unexpectedly. Her first words to me were "J'avais perdu la foi." "I have lost faith." This poem is dedicated to her and her struggle to believe after her "pearl of great price" was lost. At the same time that I received this poignant cry of her heart, the retreatants whom I was directing on the 30 day retreat were meditating on the appearances of the Risen Jesus. In the 4th "week" of the Exercises, Ignatius includes a meditation in which Jesus appears to his mother, Mary, although there is no scriptural mention of this. One of the retreatants told me that she didn't think this was necessary. "She would have known. She didn't need to see him. She would have felt his Risen presence." This inspired me to think not only of Mary's sharing the suffering of Fatima and all mothers who have lost a child but also to think of Mary's "overhearing" the Risen Jesus speaking to Mary of Magdala and the other disciples. The poem is dedicated to Fatima and Maria Rodrigues, who also lost her 17 year old son in a tragic accident two years ago.

Days Daze

Written for Friday of the 18th Week in Ordinary Time, Z's have their day.

Be Still!
19th Sunday in Ordinary Time

1 Kings 19:9-13 / Matthew 14:22-33

The explosion in the port of Beirut, Lebanon, on August 4th was just one example of the cataclysmic events that have occurred in the year 2020. The wildfires in California is another. They are woven into the fabric of this poem, the primary inspiration of which are the Theophany outside Elijah's cave and the Gospel of Jesus' walking on water and calming the storm.

Duple Time
22nd Sunday in Ordinary Time

Jerimiah 20:7-9 / Matthew 21-27

A "contretemps" is a dispute or disagreement. Jeremiah is disputing with God and Peter with Jesus in these two passages. A "contretemps" in dance is a movement that goes against time.

All's Fare
28th Sunday in Ordinary Time
ISAIAH 25:6-10/MATTHEW 22:1-14
The "banquet" is a central image in the Old and New Testament. Isaiah speaks of a banquet on God's mountain to which all nations will be invited.
The Matthean Jesus also uses the image of the banquet but in a way that challenges. One of the greatest spiritual losses during this pandemic time has been the inability to participate in the banquet of the Eucharist.

Levi-tation
Feast of St Matthew
Matthew, the tax collector, also known as Levi, was called by Jesus to get up and follow him. Matthew, the Evangelist, wove the stories of Jesus with those of Moses and Joseph, the dreamer. This poem interweaves them both.

To Know a Veil
The morning sky seemed to be a veil or curtain that could be lifted or opened at any moment. The questions became "Who's behind the curtain? Who's hidden behind the veil?"

What's Now
REVELATION 7:9-14- MATTHEW 5:1-12
The scriptures for the Solemnity of All Saints on November 1st speak of those who have survived the trial and are robed in white. In the Gospel of the Beatitudes, Jesus speaks of those who are blessed, even in their suffering and loss.

Enthralled
As we came to the end of the liturgical year with the Solemnity of Christ King of the Universe, the question came to be "In whose thrall are you?" Who has power over you? Is it Christ, or the World with all its woes?

And How!
Feast of the Immaculate Conception
The final poem in this collection was written for the feast in honor of Mary, the mother of Jesus, who asked the question, "And how can this be?" The answer is found in an exclamation point. And How!

ABOUT THE AUTHOR

Robert VerEecke is a Jesuit priest who presently serves on the staff of retreat directors at Gonzaga Eastern Point Retreat House in Gloucester, Massachusetts. Fr VerEecke began his ordained ministry at Boston College in 1978 as a member of the Chaplaincy staff. He was appointed Jesuit Artist-in-Residence in 1982, working in the Theater Department and the University Chaplaincy. During that time, he founded the Boston Liturgical Dance Ensemble. He is widely known known for his work in the integration of dance and religious expression and is co-author of *Introducing Dance in Christian Worship* (Pastoral Press 1999). For 27 years, Fr.VerEecke served as pastor of St Ignatius Church on the Campus of Boston College.

ACKNOWLEDGEMENTS

I am more than grateful to the staff and retreatants of Gonzaga Eastern Point Retreat house for their support for this project and appreciation for these poems, which are inspired by the place and people who come to pray on this Holy Ground. I am also most grateful to the Board of the Boston Liturgical Dance Ensemble, the dance company I have directed for 40 years as well as donors of the company. Their financial and personal support have made this project possible.

A special thanks to Fr. William Campbell SJ, director of Gonzaga Eastern Point Retreat House and Fr Randy Sachs SJ for their dedication to our shared ministry.

A special thanks to Fr. JA Loftus SJ for his encouragement for this work and to Dr. Anthony Compagnone who helped with the editing of the manuscript.

A special thanks to poets Gerard Manley Hopkins, Mary Oliver, and Paul Mariani for their inspiration.

A special thanks to the staff of Paraclete Press for their care and assistance in bringing this work to fruition.

And a very special thanks to the Divine Marksman who has always set my soul aquiver!

Made in the USA
Middletown, DE
22 April 2022